Guide to The Beautiful and Historic Lucerne Valley and Vicinity

Volume 5

by William Jack Mann
A.K.A. Shortfuse

Shortfuse Publishing Co.
30 Hilltop Terrace
Barstow, California 92311

Guide to The Beautiful and Historic Lucerne Valley and Vicinity

Volume 5

by William Jack Mann

Shortfuse Publishing Co.
30 Hilltop Terrace
Barstow, CA 92311
USA

©2003 by William J. Mann
All Rights Reserved
Set in 11 point Romana BT and Times type
Book Design and Layout by:
Dick Tristao's TwoBitGrafix
Visalia, California
TwoBitGrafix@Comcast.net
Original Cover Design by Dave Tisthammer
Cover photo by Steven Rohn
Printed by Jostens, Inc., Commercial Department
Visalia, California

ISBN 9667947-4-5

DEDICATION

I want to dedicate volume five, to my new found friends, Bill and Jan Lembright. Without Bill's energy, push, and determination, there never would have been a Lucerne Valley Guide Book.

I must confess that at first, I was not enthusiastic but Bill kept after me, until I did get fired up. We have spent many hours together on the desert.

I am pleased to call this very dedicated couple my friends.

PREFACE

The Lucerne Valley area is huge and very different. It goes from high desert mountains to very low, sandy valleys and large dry lakes. It is a mostly open area with many roads and trails and it is very difficult to give directions. I still use GPS and the DeLorme, Southern and Central California Atlas and Gazetter road map book. Because of the sand, as well as many roads and trails, I am doing this book a little different on the road directions. I made a map with the location of sites, numbered, so you can find them a little easier. Between GPS, DeLorme, and the map, I think you should find the sites. If you can't find them, I guarantee you will have a good time looking for them. You might find another, equally exciting site! Remember: the weather can change on a moments notice and the wind can be brutal, so it is very important that you follow my warnings!

Photo by Steven Rohn   Art by Rocky Johnson

ACKNOWLEDGEMENTS

I have had lots of help from many people on my Volume Five Guide Book. I want to thank my pal, Don Taylor, for the hours he spent chauffeuring me. He took hundreds of pictures and helped me in numerous ways.

There would not have been a Lucerne Valley guide book if it had not been for the efforts of Bill Lembright with help from his wife, Jan. He made the map of the sites, took pictures, and guided us on many of the Monday trips - his day off. He was responsible for getting the aircraft wreck site into the book, as well as many other sites.

Derald Francis, I call him the Lucerne Valley guide service, guided us to most sites in the book and furnished his own four wheeled drive vehicle so we would always have two vehicles if we got into trouble. He never would accept any help on the gas. He was always fun to be around and we have developed a great friendship.

Fran Elgin helped me with pictures at Victor Valley College. Longtime friend, Carolyn Clark, did lots of research and was a great help in furnishing me historical research material.

Chuck and Marjorie Valenzuela gave us a great tour of their Granite Mountain Railroad and museum. Dorothy and John Ligouri were very helpful at Rabbit Springs and The Hangman's Tree.

Mr. And Mrs. Bob McDougall furnished us with great old newspapers and pictures. Pat Eblen furnished us with information and pictures of the plane that crashed. Cliff Palmer loaned us a great photo album of pictures he took while he worked at Camp Rock. He took the picture of the beautiful sunset over Lucerne Valley which I used in the book.

I want to thank Charles Smith (Smitty) for the great tour of Camp Rock. I would like to thank Bill Wilson for being our Johnson Valley tour guide. He showed us some great sites besides guiding us to Willie Boy's Grave.

My friend, Doug Schumway, gave me information and research material about Cushenbury Springs and the Black Hawk area. Ernie, Barbara, and Linda Gommel gave me advice and encouragement. Barbara Veal and her daughter, Millie Rader, went on several trips. And Rocky Johnson for his great cartoons.

Chuck Rader gave us a great tour of the Lucerne Valley Museum. We had a great tour of Old Woman Springs led by Bob Humphrey. The following either provided pictures or went with us: Dick Clark, Donna Chandler, George Jones, John Masse, Don Cox, Bill Zualet. Gary Grant for the Verde Antique Marble Sphere and Bookends.

Troy and Betty Reed, Bill Lattin, Allen Stanfield, Al and Janet Miller, Lynne Hilton, Bill and Carolyn Russell, all loaned us great pictures. Martha Coutant loaned us wonderful pictures of Rabbit Springs, and her book on the Heart Bar Ranch was a great help. A must read for every one who is interested in the area.

Will and Darlene Garrett showed us the goat on goat mountain. I want to thank Don Judkins for the help on the One Ton Mine and George Carmona for his help on Jim Hill's Treasure Chest and Mine. I appreciate the help of Andy Anderson about the Cement Boat. Ken Schmidt helped us on the Silver Reef Mine. Al Filippi helped us on the Box S Ranch. Dora Moon, as well as Pete and Freda Leibrick were a great help about the El Sueno Arrastra and Guest Ranch. Jim Goldsworthy gave us information concerning the Lucerne Lake cracks and rocket site. Ruth Whitcavitch gave us the story on the Dinosaur House and Mark Riddle with the Eagle Scouts and friends repaired and cleaned it up. Paul and Renee Longshore went on several trips and took great pictures.

Steven Rohn, my grandson, took the great picture we are using for the cover. He took other pictures and helped us on the computer.

I want to thank my daughter, Julie Mann Clemmer, for continuing to handle credit card and Internet sales.

Last, but not least, I want to thank my wife and buddy of fifty years, Dottie, for the many hours of proof reading and computer work she did for Volume Five.

WARNING!!

Traveling unprepared in the vast Mojave Desert could be hazardous to your health. Please read the following instructions before venturing out into the great unknown.

Old Mine Shafts. The Mojave Desert is a treasure trove of almost every mineral and gemstone known. It has been mined heavily for about two hundred years. It is filled with thousands of mine shafts that beckon to be explored. DON'T! If you want to climb down, be sure you have a stout rope around you and held by a strong person who belongs to the same political party! I don't recommend that this person be your mother-in-law! If you still insist on climbing down old mine shafts, okay, because Barstow has a good search and rescue squad that needs practice retrieving bodies from mine shafts.

Rattlesnakes. I carry a snake stick and keep it ahead of me at all times. I have been struck at numerous times and even chased by a mean sidewinder! Yes, they can spring clear off the ground. It is amazing how agile you can be when one is hot on your posterior. The hotter it is, the meaner they are. The sidewinder should be the logo for the IRS! Seriously, you should always be careful where you put your hands and feet. If struck, head for the nearest hospital, keeping the area as cold as possible. Snakebite kits are still sold but the best recommendation is to get to a hospital as quick as you can.

Weather. Disregard all weather forecasts. Dad Fairbanks, the famous rancher and miner from Shoshone and Greenwater, said years ago that anyone who tries to predict the weather in the desert is either a greenhorn or a damn fool. Be prepared for everything. If you get into a cloudburst or sandstorm, don't be surprised. It is not a disaster if you are prepared. It is an adventure! I have never had a disaster on the desert, but plenty of adventures!

Water. When you go into the back country make sure you have plenty of water, cold beer and a bag of bones. In the early days I carried a bag of carrots too. People who live in isolated areas are usually not very friendly. They are out there for a reason. The common medium of exchange is beer. I have been greeted with a cold stare by a gun-toting hermit and was once greeted by a shot overhead. Without a word, I reach into my ice chest and handed over a cold beer. In this way, I make life-long friends of desert characters. They always have at least one dog. I toss Rover a couple of bones and we are buddies for life. Surprisingly, the burro is still present. He is a prized companion and friend so I give him a carrot. They all have good memories and it is fun to drive up the second time and see the old prospector, dog, and the burro start salivating at the same time when they recognize me. By the way, if you get marooned in the desert and run out of water, you can party on the beer and chew on the bones and the carrots! This is called survival.

Compatible Traveling Companion. Always have a second vehicle besides the usual cell phone, tools and camping gear. Make sure each vehicle has plenty of gas and enough food and water to survive several days if need be. (If both vehicles break down, you can party on the beer and survive on the bones and carrots. Heck! You may not want to be rescued!

How Shortfuse Got His Name

In the early years of our business, both Ron Brubaker and I had blasting licenses. When we started in 1950, the rock business was slow getting started so we took all sorts of odd jobs to keep food on the table. Some of these jobs included blasting. People who did blasting were scarce on the high desert so we were asked to do all kinds of jobs. For example, I blew up two railroad bridges and fortunately got the right ones; blasted set-up concrete inside redi-mix trucks; broke up concrete inside buildings; shot numerous wells to shake up the scale on the intake valves and many other jobs.

One of the jobs using dynamite was to carefully shake-up the concrete on an arrastra that the Mojave River Valley Museum was relocating from an isolated gold mine. This included many small blasts using timed fuses. There were many movie cameras trained on the blast site. The blasts went off before I said they would and the cameramen were annoyed. Someone said, "We'll just call you 'Shortfuse' from now on." The name stuck and then they started calling my wife, Dottie, "Dynamite", and that name stuck too. Anyway, it has been fun.

Contents

Dedication iii
Preface iv
Acknowledgements v
WARNING!! vi
How Shortfuse Got His Name vi

INTRODUCTION 1
MAP 2
01 GOLD BELT MINE 4
02 ONE TON MINE 6
03 JIM HILL'S TREASURE CHEST 7
04 WWII BOMB TARGETS 10
05 QUILL SPRINGS 13
06 TYLER VALLEY INDIAN CIRCLES 14
07 HERCULES FINGER 16
08 YUCCA RINGS 18
09 FRY MOUNTAIN GOLD MINES 19
10 FORD AND GRANDVIEW GOLD MINES 22
11 ORD BELT GOLD MINE 24
12 JOJOBA BUSHES AND MAUMEE MINE 26
13 COPPER STRAND MINE 27
14 CAMP ROCK MINE 28
15 TEXAS QUARRY 30
16 KING CLONE 32
17 COUGAR BUTTES 33
18 GREEN ROCK QUARRY-DESERT JADE 36
19 CEMENT BOAT 38
20 EARTHQUAKE ESCARPMENT 39
21 SILVER CLIFF-SILVER BELLE MINES 40
22 SAND DUNES OF JOHNSON VALLEY 42
23 EMERSON GOLD MINE 43
24 BESSEMER IRON MINE 44
25 WILLY BOY'S GRAVE 45
26 INTEGRETRON 46
27 GIANT ROCK 49
28 GUBLER ORCHIDS 50

#	Entry	Page
29	JOHNSON VALLEY PETROGLYPHS-BOOTH'S FOLLY	52
30	ROCK CORRAL	54
31	OLD WOMAN SPRINGS	55
32	LESTER DALE MINE	58
33	BLACKHAWK GOLD MINE and MILL	60
34	BLACKHAWK LANDSLIDE	61
35	SILVER REEF MINE	62
36	HOT GLASS RANCH	64
37	GOBAR'S DAIRY	65
38	RABBIT SPRINGS-HANGMAN'S TREE	66
39	PETER DAVISDON'S GRAVE	68
40	BOX S RANCH	69
41	RANCHO EL SUENO-ARRASTRA	70
42	WOLF MOUNTAIN SANCTUARY	72
43	CUSHENBERRY SPRINGS	74
44	GRANITE MOUNTAIN RAILROAD	76
45	A4 AIRCRAFT CRASH	78
46	VERDE ANTIQUE	79
47	DEEP CREEK HOT SPRINGS	80
48a	LUCERNE EARTHQUAKE CRACKS	82
48b	LUCERNE MODEL ROCKET SITE	83
49	DINOSAUR HOUSE	84
50	WORM RACE	86
51	SAWTOOH CANYON	87
52	GOAT MOUNTAIN	88
53	LUCERNE MUSEUM	89
54	CHIMNEY ROCK	90
55	HITCHHIKER'S THUMB	91
	THE DESERT IN BLOOM	92
	SPONSORS	93
	CLOSING and GALLERY	96
	ABOUT THE AUTHOR	108

LUCERNE VALLEY
and Vicinity

INTRODUCTION

I have been interested in the Lucerne Valley area for a very long time. I first came with my father's Boy Scout Troop 7, in the late 1930's and early 1940's.

We camped, explored, and had a great time. After World War II, I prospected, hauled decorative rock, camped, and explored the area.

In 2002, I decided to do a guide book of the Valley and started doing research. I saw unusual sites in the back country, usually guided by Derald Francis or Bill Lembright. What I found was extremely interesting. The many homestead ruins tell of the hardships and struggles of homesteaders in the Great Depression. The mines tell the hardship and sweat that the old miners went to in their search of wealth. Lucerne Valley is proud of its characters, both past and present. These kinds of people made our country the great country that it is today.

I am attempting to show you as many of these interesting sites as possible. I hope you will enjoy Lucerne Valley and vicinity as much as I have.

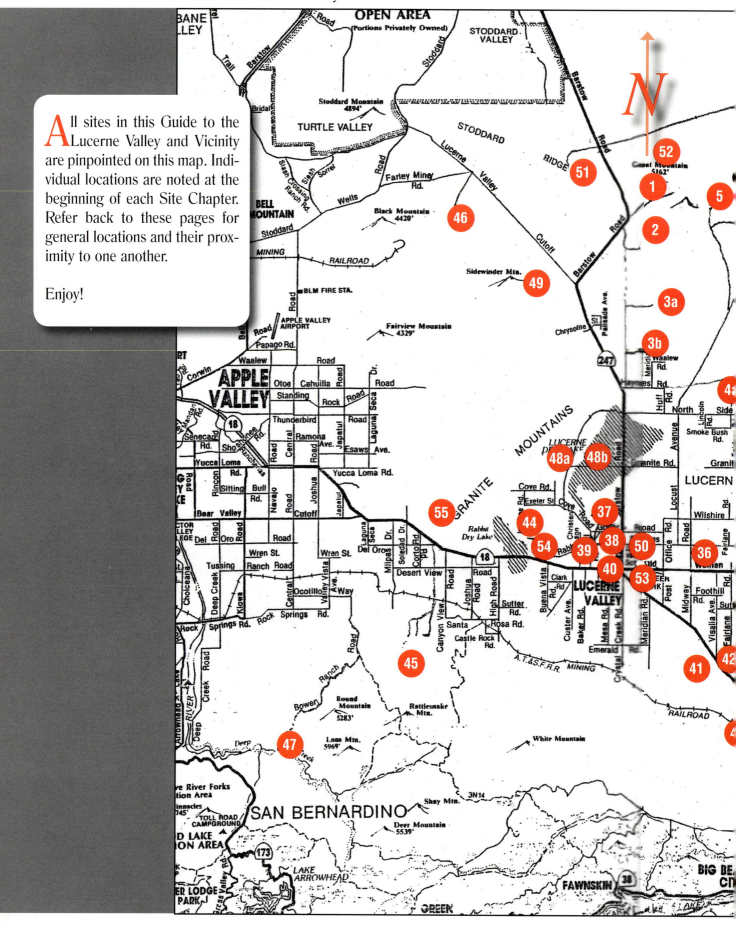

All sites in this Guide to the Lucerne Valley and Vicinity are pinpointed on this map. Individual locations are noted at the beginning of each Site Chapter. Refer back to these pages for general locations and their proximity to one another.

Enjoy!

Lucerne Valley and Vicinity

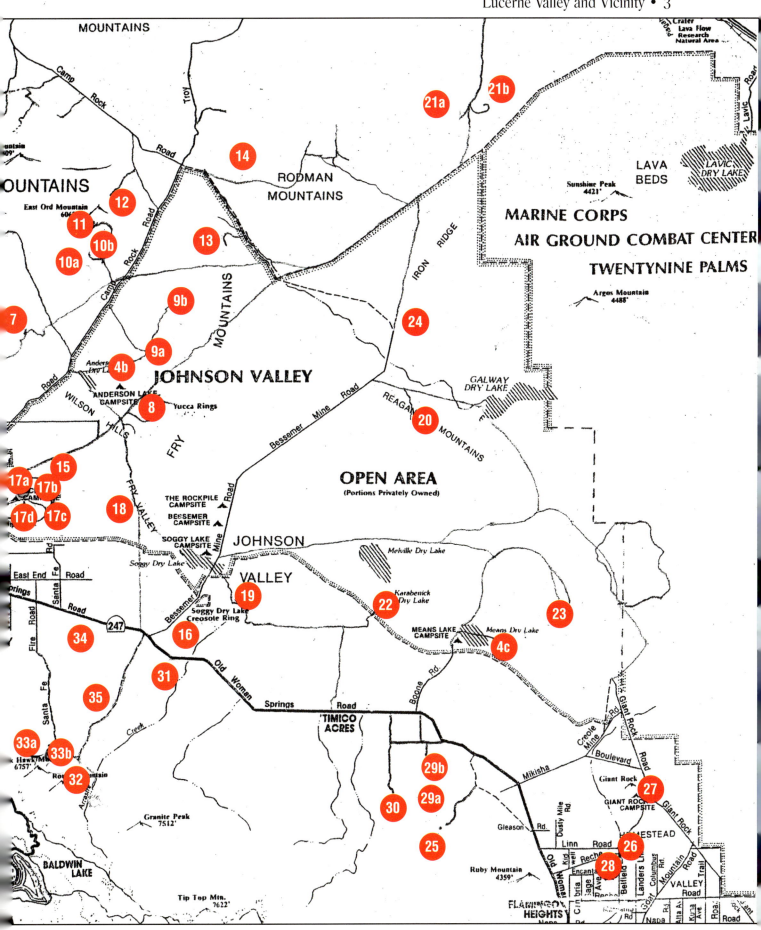

Gold Belt Gold Mine

High on the side of the mountain in the West Ord Mountain area and not too far from the Goat Mountain Pass on Highway 247, is the Gold Belt gold mine. It is a good sized gold mine and had a forty ton per day processing mill on site. It operated from 1930 to 1932, and has been idle since. The mill has been removed but there are extensive slabs and foundations besides housing sites. The ore samples are pretty and I originally thought it was a copper mine because the ore shows chalcopyrite, a copper mineral. There are three levels high on the mountain and in the trail are large patches of this turquoise colored copper mineral. Watch out for diamond backs as we ran into two of them on the trail between the levels. A very interesting place with great views. Enjoy!

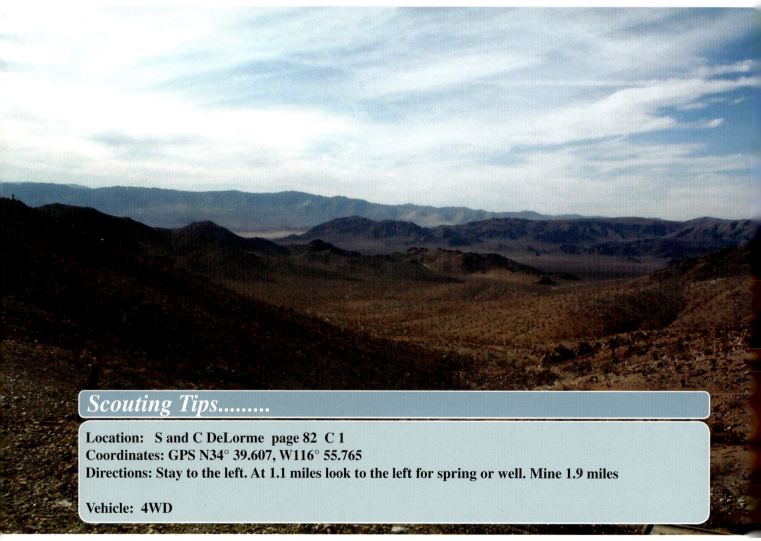

Scouting Tips.........

Location: S and C DeLorme page 82 C 1
Coordinates: GPS N34° 39.607, W116° 55.765
Directions: Stay to the left. At 1.1 miles look to the left for spring or well. Mine 1.9 miles

Vehicle: 4WD

Gold Belt Gold Mine • 5

Top: Gold Belt Mine Mill site. Above; Gold Ore.

Far left; View of valley from the mine site. Left; Jan Lembright taking five.

One Ton Mine

A short distance off of Highway 247, approximately halfway between Lucerne Valley and Barstow, there is a large area of mining activities. I can't find out much about this area, but there are several concrete mill sites and lots of scattered ruins, indicating much mining activity. It is not far off the pavement and a great place to explore. I would not go in the mines, but there is plenty to explore on the surface. There are also signs of recent gold mining and processing. You can even camp on some of the slabs.

View from the mine.

Scouting Tips.........

Location: DeLorme page 82 C 1
Coordinates: GPS N34° 37.394, W116° 56.450

Vehicle: 2WD High Clearance, Good Campsites.

Jim Hill's Treasure Chest and Gold Mine

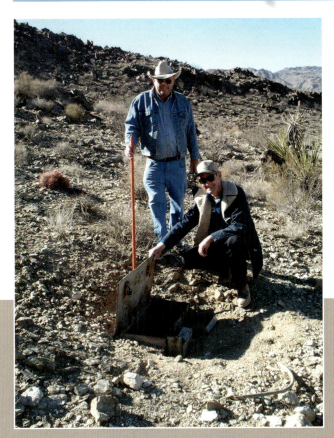

Two months before he died, Jim Hill said that he had discovered a metal chest with two padlocks and anchored in rock. He was full of stories and exaggerations, but what a mystery! We decided to check it out. We searched and searched, but found no chest. The site was scoured with metal detectors, to no avail.

About a year later, while scouting around Jim's place, Derald Francis said "Let me show you a metal box I found embedded in concrete". From his description, I knew it had to be Jim's chest! It had been pried open and the contents gone. What a mystery! Who did it and why? This mystery was told to me by Bill Lembright. Enjoy!

Above: The author and Derald Francis.

Right; The fabled Treasure Chest

Scouting Tips: Jim Hill's Treasure Chest ....

Location: DeLorme page 82 C 1
Coordinates: GPS N340° 35.717, W160° 56.402
Directions: From corner of Hwys 247 and 18, go north on 247, seven miles to Haynes Road. At 7.2 miles, jog left on Fern Road. At ten miles turn right on a faint dirt road. At 10.3 miles, park. Look for metal chest in ground fifty yards southeast by Yucca clump. South, about three hundred yards over a low hill, is Jim Hill's cabin.

Vehicle: 4WD

Jim Hill's Treasure Chest and Gold Mine....continued.

Above; Site of Jim Hill's mining camp. Bus was his home until cabin was built.

Art by Rocky Johnson

Author and Derald Francis. Note J.H. on overhead beam.

Jim Hill's Treasure Chest and Gold Mine • 9

Left; Jim Hill's initials carved into the beam.

Ore sample from the mine site

Light circle area above is location of Jim Hill's Mine, a few miles north-westerly from his home site.

Scouting Tips.........Jim Hill Mine

Location: DeLorme page 82 C 1
Coordinates: GPS N34° 35.717, W116° 56.066
Directions: Jim Hill mine location: look high on mountain for mine dump and road leading to it. Also look for ruins of stone cabins and look for pretty rock specimens at the mine entrance and dump.

Vehicle: 4WD

World War II Bomb Targets

During World War II, the Mojave Desert was heavily used for training purposes and military maneuvers. There were a series of ground targets set up for flyers to practice their bombing skills. Lucerne Valley was chosen for numerous ground targets because of its remoteness. It was close to airfields so the planes would not have to fly long distances to these targets. They were usually made of a bullseye of black asphalt circles with a pile of white rock in the center. Many bomb fragments remain and, although they are over fifty years old, I would not handle them. Enjoy!

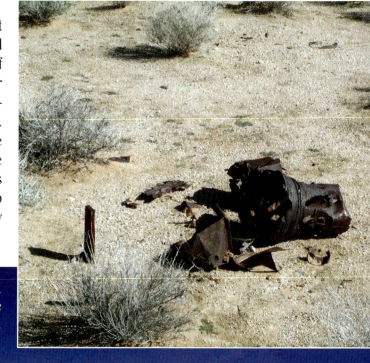

*Right; Bomb fragments.
Below; Pavement rings form the target.*

World War II Bomb Targets • 11

Left; Author by some of the bomb fragments, Below; one of the bullseyes. Use caution around the fragments, do not handle them.

Scouting Tips: Fairlane Bomb Target.........

Location: DeLorme page 82 D1
Coordinates: GPS: N 34 Degrees 32.715 W 116 Degrees 52.475
Directions: 1.1 miles north of Northside Road on Fairlane Road
Vehicle: 2WD

Scouting Tips: Anderson Dry Lake Target.........

Location: DeLorme page 82 D 2
Coordinates: GPS: N 34 degrees 33.588   W 116 degrees 45.372

Vehicle: 4WD

Scouting Tips: Mean's Dry Lake Target.........

Location: DeLorme page 97 A 4.5
Coordinates: GPS: N 34 degrees 23.854 W 116 degrees 29.569
Directions: from four corners in Lucerne Valley east on Hwy 247, 25 miles to Boone Road, north 5.1 miles to Mean's Dry Lake, bear east 2 miles around Mean's Lake to target.
Vehicle: 4WD

High in a remote canyon between Goat Mountain and West Ord Mountain is a hidden spring. It is a beautiful area with spectacular rock formations. In the springtime, the flowers are great. Because water is precious, this site shows signs of ancient habitation in the form of Indian petroglyphs, hunting blinds, and bedrock grinding metates. There are also signs that early prospectors camped there leaving soldered cans and cleared campsites. Please do not touch the petroglyphs. Remember, disturbing relics of any kind is a serious offense. It is a beautiful but rough camping area. Enjoy, but please leave it cleaner than when you came.

One of the old springs

Quill Springs

One of the Petroglyphs at Quill Springs.

Scouting Tips.........

Location: DeLorme page 82 c 1.5
Coordinates: GPS: N 34 degrees 38.633 W 116 degrees 53.411
Directions: From corner of 247 & 18, go East 5 miles. Turn left on Camp Rock Rd. Continue straight on Harrod Rd. (BLM OM7) for 20.7 miles to BLM OM30. Turn left for 1.6 miles, then bear left 2.4 miles to locked gate.
Vehicle: 4WD

14 • Bill Mann's Guide to the Lucerne Valley

Tyler Valley Indian Circles

MAP 06

On top of a saddle overlooking Tyler Valley on the southwest side of East Ord Mountain, are two mysterious Indian Circles. They are mysterious because they seem to me to be too big for sleeping circles. What are they? There is a well defined trail leading out of Tyler Valley to these circles. Please do not disturb the circles. Remember, it is a serious offense to disturb any artifacts. Beautiful views and good camping in the area. Enjoy!

Author on trail to Indian Circles

Scouting Tips.........

Location: DeLorme page 82 C 2

Coordinates: GPS: N 34 degrees 38.138 W 116 degrees 50.408

Directions: Turn off is 8.8 miles from Daryll's house. Turn left on OM 30, bear left 6.0 miles to Tyler Dry Lake (a good place to camp). Go 6.6 miles and take right fork.

Vehicle: 2WD High Clearance

Tyler Valley Indian Circles/Lucerne Valley Bits • 15

Bits from Lucerne Valley's Past....

"You were right, Oscar, I should have done my shopping in Lucerne Valley."

Lucerne Valley Leader Ads and cartoons, Courtesy of Mr. & Mrs. Bob McDougall

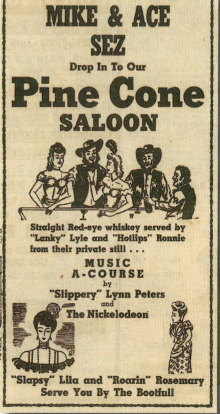

16 • Bill Mann's Guide to the Lucerne Valley
Hercules' Finger

MAP 07

On the southern flank of the Ord Mountains there is an awesome granite pinnacle that sticks up on the skyline. It is in an area of giant granite boulders that contain rock shelters showing signs of early occupation. Did these early Americans come here to worship this magnificent natural wonder? I marveled at it and I think you will too. Pack it in, pack it out and enjoy!

Author at Balance Rock near Hercules' Finger.

Scouting Tips.........

Location: DeLorme page 82 C 2.5
Coordinates: GPS: N 34 degrees 35.049
W 116 degrees 48.699

Vehicle: 4WD

Hercules' Finger • 17

Hercules' Finger is a popular challenge for climbers.

18 • Bill Mann's Guide to the Lucerne Valley

Yucca Rings

Alongside the power line road in the Fry Mountain area, are some almost perfect rings of Yucca bushes. Each of these rings is reputed to have started from a single bush thousands of years ago. Each of these bushes came from a single host and is a perfect clone of the original bush. The rings are precious and have been fenced to protect them. There is good camping in the area. Beautiful views. Enjoy!

Scouting Tips.........

Location: DeLorme page 96 A 3
Coordinates: GPS: N 34 degrees 32.081 W 116 degrees 43.491
Directions: About 2 miles east of Cougar Flats on Transmission Line Road.

Vehicle: 2WD High Clearance

Fry Mountain Gold Mines continued...

High in the Fry Mountains are a number of old gold mines that show considerable use and age. One of these mines contains a very unusual arrastra in good condition. This arrastra has a very large wooden wheel that drags the drag stones around the circle, crushing the ore. It is in near perfect condition. I have never seen one like this. I marvel about the ability of these old miners to produce machines like this one. There are also several concrete millsites and dwelling areas with purple glass shards indicating age. This wheel is precious so please do not disturb it and let other people enjoy it. Enjoy!

Looking down from the mine.

Scouting Tips.........

Location: DeLorme page 82 D 2.5
Coordinates: GPS: N 34 degrees 34.863 W 116 degrees 43.375

Vehicle: 4WD

Fry Mountain Gold Mines

Fry Mountain Gold Mines • 21

Large photo; Arrastra on the site.
Far left; Author near the Arrastra.
Left; View inside of Arrastra shows wear on the stones.
Top; Dated rock carvings near the mine.
Above; Possible Indian Circle close to the mine.

22 • Bill Mann's Guide to the Lucerne Valley

Ford Gold Mine and Grand View Gold Mine

MAP 10a,b

Scouting Tips.........

Location: DeLorme page 82 C 2.5
Coordinates: GPS: Ford Mine: N 34 degrees 37.271 W 116 degrees 45.799 Digital 581-587
                Grand View Mine: N 34 degrees 37.219 W 116 degrees 45.328
Directions: See Ord Mine.

Vehicle: 4WD

Ford and Grand View Gold Mines

High on the south slope of East Ord Mountain, are two mining areas. They are close enough that I decided to make them one site. At the Ford Mine there are many interesting drill pad sights and awesome valley views. There are numerous mines with beautiful gold ore samples. In the canyon below, there is interesting mining debris. Great camping with awesome views of the valley. Remember: stay out of the mines and stay alive!! At the Grand View Gold Mine, which is around the mountain to the east and within sight, is another collection of mines and mill site ruins plus living areas. The main point of interest at the Grand View is the existence of "Bugeye Rhyolite". It is in outcroppings just above the mill and on the hillside above the old mine. The unusual specimens are very abundant. A great place for rockhounds looking for cutting material. Great campsites with great views. Enjoy!

Signs of old mining camp.

Lucerne Valley Leader Ad, Jan. 10, 1957
Courtesy of Mr. & Mrs. Bob McDougall

Ord Belt Gold Mine

High on the southeast slope of East Ord Mountain is the Ord Belt Gold Mine. There are extensive workings in this area with the ruins of a tramway coming down from some of the higher workings. As you approach the main mine, there is a concrete guzzler for wildlife on your right. It is meant to channel the water into a cistern and save it for the critters of the area. There are numerous signs of habitation going back a long way. There are also signs of fairly recent drilling activities in the area. You can see Squaw Tea, ruins of an arrastra, and pretty ore samples. A very interesting and beautiful place. Enjoy!

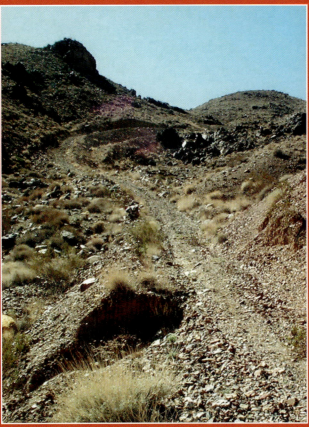
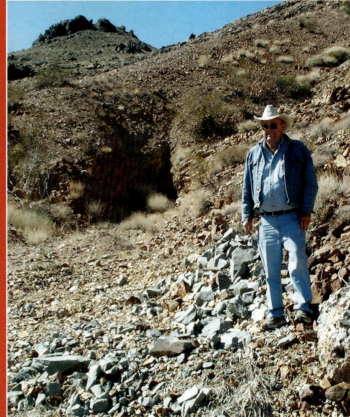

Scouting Tips.........

Location: DeLorme page 82 C 2.5
Coordinates: GPS: N 34 degrees 37.625 W 116 degrees 45.427

Vehicle: Extreme four wheel drive

Top left on opposite page; Derald Francis and Guzzler. Above; Author and Derald Francis at mine ruins. Left; Derald Francis in old foundation of miner's quarters.

Jojoba Bushes and the Maumee Mine

Jojoba Bushes and the Maumee Mine are on the northerly slope of East Ord Mountain. The bushes are a large group and are somewhat rare. This patch has been fenced to protect it. Jojoba Bushes have thick, oily leaves and small yellow flowers complete with a berry. The bushes are about six feet tall and are reputed to have been used by Indians for medicinal purposes. Some call them the Goat Nut Bushes. The scientific name is Semmondsia Chinensis.

The road continues past the bushes to the historic Maumee Mine. The road is in very bad condition, but once there, you are treated to a trip back in history and an awesome view.

This site is close to Willis Well which is on page 61 of my volume I

Scouting Tips.........

Location: DeLorme page 82 C 2.5
Coordinates: GPS: N 34 degrees 39.721 W 116 degrees 44.781. Maumee Mine is on hill side due south of the fenced bushes
Vehicle: 4WD

Jojoba Bushes and the Maumee Mine/Copper Strand Mine

Copper Strand Mine

Possible old Indian trail trail through the area.

High on the northeast slope of the Fry Mountains and east of Camp Rock Mine is the Copper Strand Mine. It first opened in 1900, during the copper boom, when the United States was being electrified. The last production was in 1940. I have a personal interest in this mine because my parents were friends of the owner, L.P. Haney. My father brought our Boy Scout Troop here from Pomona, for a campout. That was just before World War II, in 1941. Mr. Haney suggested that we hang our hunting knife blades in the solution of copper and cyanide overnight and they would be copper plated. We did this and the blades were plated! When visiting the site to write this story, I was astounded to see the little wire and board where we hung our knives at the edge of the tank over sixty years ago, still hanging right there. This is a great place to explore with interesting rock samples to gather and a quaint rock house to check out. There is also a well traveled Indian path that crosses the property below the old mill ruins. Enjoy!

Tank where Author's knife was copper plated

Above middle; Jan Lembright at cabin entrance. Above, Author at rock cabin.

Scouting Tips.........

Location: DeLorme page 82 D 3
Coordinates: GPS: N 34 degrees 37.880 W 116 degrees 40.026

Vehicle: 4WD

Camp Rock Mine

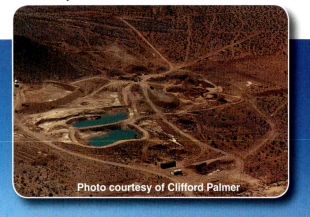
Camp Rock Gold Mine in the 1980's.
Photo courtesy of Clifford Palmer

MAP 14

Camp Rock Mine is a famous placer mine in alluvium (sand and gravel). The gold is usually fine grained but some nuggets have been found. It was worked by dry washing prior to 1932. In 1932, a well was put down and a washing and screening plant installed. After a short run it completely shut down. The latest production was in 1980, when a large well was put down and a dependable water supply was found. A large wet plant was installed. It operated on and off for several years as investors came and went. It was never able to return a regular profit and finally shut down for good in the late 1980's. It is a private property owned by my friend, Charles Smith of Lucerne Valley. Smitty is a good guy and said he would give permission for people to dry wash but he wants them to ask before they start. A great place to explore with good camping and good views. Pack it in, pack it out. His telephone number is 760-248-7190. Enjoy!

Scouting Tips.........

Location: DeLorme page 82 C 3
Coordinates: GPS: N 34 degrees 40.143 W 116 degrees 48.298

Vehicle: 2WD High Clearance

Camp Rock Mining maching, 1980's
Photo courtesy of Clifford Palmer

Camp Rock Mine • 29

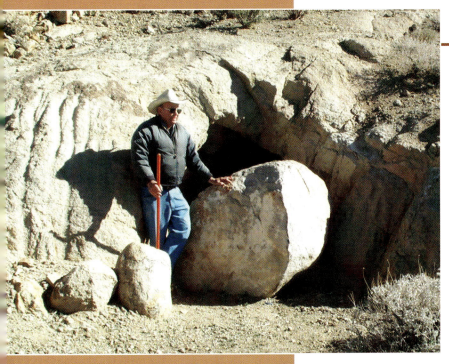

Locket with gold nugget found at the mine.

Cliff Palmer, Author Bill Mann and C. (Smitty) Smith

Texas Quarry

About ten miles east, northeast of Lucerne Valley town and just east of Cougar Buttes is the Texas quarry. Mostly worked in the 1930's for granite building stone for building facings and monuments, it continued production as late as 1950, providing stone for construction of buildings at the University of California, both at Los Angeles and La Jolla. The stone was quarried in big blocks, ten to twenty feet long, and then trucked to the finishing location. There it was cut into desired sizes and polished. The color is gray to yellowish gray. The product was called Golden Vein Granite. There still are huge blocks ready to be shipped. It is an awesome sight to see the amount of work these miners went to getting these huge blocks of granite to the market. A great area to explore, and for camping and views. Enjoy!

Scouting Tips.........

Location: DeLorme page 96 A 2
Coordinates: GPS: N 34 degrees 29.932 W 116 degrees 47.686

Vehicle: 4WD

Upper left; Notice the drill holes. Left; Quite a view of Lucerne Valley from the quarry

Some of these blocks are enormous. Notice in left middle photo the size compared to a full size vehicle.

King Clone

Alongside the Bessemer Mine Road are circles of Creosote bushes. The early miners often called them greasewood because of their oily content. The early Americans used their oil and leaves for medicinal purposes and their limbs for warmth because they made such a hot fire. They also made their wicki-ups (brush shelters) from the limbs. This circle grew from a single host plant. As the bush grew outward, the center of the plant would die. The result would be a huge ring of cloned bushes dating many thousands of years old. Please respect these ancient bushes. These may be the oldest living things on earth!! Enjoy!

Art by Rocky Johnson

Scouting Tips.........

Location: DeLorme page 96 A 3
Coordinates: GPS: N 34 degrees 25.233 W 116 degrees 42.245
Directions: 1.5 miles from Highway 247, on the Bessemer Mine Road and seventy-five to one hundred yards east. Look for rock cairns on the right.

Vehicle: 2WD

King Clone/Cougar Buttes • 33

MAP 17 a,b,c,d,e

Cougar Buttes
More...

Cougar Buttes is an awesome line of impressive piles of granite like boulders cutting diagonally across eastern Lucerne Valley. They must have come up out of the earth's crust along a fault untold millions of years ago. Because of the roughness of the Buttes, and the many places to hide, it was reputed to be the home of numerous Cougars or Mountain Lions in the old days. That roughness made it an ideal place for ancient man to camp. Many of the numerous rock shelters show signs of his past presence. It is a great place to family camp and explore. There is one beautiful view after another. You can explore the many rock formations and dream up all kinds of names. I am including five great ones, but know there are many more: A. The Arches. B. The Indian ball room. (where I fell) C. Two rock Shelter. D. Jaws cave. E. Sphinx Rock. Please pack it in and pack it out This is a beautiful area.. Enjoy!

Scouting Tips.........

Location: DeLorme page 96 A 2

Coordinates:
   Site A The Arches
      N 34 degrees 29.349 W 116 degrees 49.239
   Site B: The Indian ball room. (where I fell)
      N 24 degrees 29.417 W 116 degrees 47.678
   Site C: Two rock Shelters
      N 34 degrees 28.417 W 116 degrees 47.227
   Site D: Jaws Cave
      N 34 degrees 28.486 W 116 degrees 48.188
   Site E: Sphinx Rock
      N 34 degrees 28.496 W 116 degrees 49.579

Vehicle: 4 WD

34 • Bill Mann's Guide to the Lucerne Valley
Cougar Buttes...Continued.

Above; A striking view from inside Indian Ballroom. Far right at top of page; Derald Francis stands where Author fell in the Indian Ballroom. Far right middle; Jaw's Cave. Far right; The Arches. Right; Sphinx Rock.

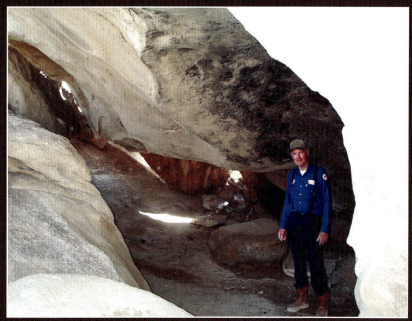

Green Rock Quarry - Home of Desert Jade

On the southern slope of the Fry Mountains and westerly from Soggy Dry Lake is a green rock quarry. A rock that is green all the way through is quite rare, and to have it hard enough to take and keep a polish is really rare. Rock hounds call it Desert Jade, and it indeed looks very much like real jade. This rock is called a silicious epidote, the color coming from copper. The bulk of the rock is silica which gives it its hardness. Most of the mining was since World War II and was for the decorative rock market – roofing granules and landscaping rock. It was mined in at least two different eras. Great scenic views. Enjoy!

Scouting Tips.........

Location: Directions: DeLorme page 96 A 2.5
Coordinates: GPS: N 34 degrees 29.581 W 116 degrees 43.320

Vehicle: 4 WD

Green Rock Quarry - Home of Desert Jade • 37

The Cement Boat

MAP 19

O n a beautiful, abandoned ranch site complete with large shade trees, is one of the true mysteries of the Lucerne Valley area. It is a large, ocean going, plastered ship. It is upside down on house moving dollies. The boat is approximately fifty feet long and about two stories tall. I crawled under it, and it is beautifully and meticulously built. It is almost finished. Someone spent a lot of time and money before abandoning it. I wondered how he ever figured on getting it set upright and launched. Please respect this private property and don't remove anything. Enjoy and wonder as I have.

Jan Lembright (top) and Author (above) provide size comparison to the cement boat.

Scouting Tips.........

Location: DeLorme page 96 A 3
Coordinates: GPS: N 34 degrees 25.626 W 116 degrees 40.843

Vehicle: 2WD

The Cement Boat/Earthquake Escarpment • 39

MAP 20 Earthquake Escarpment

Derald Francis at the Escarpment.

In 1992, during the violent Landers earthquake in upper Johnson Valley the earth ruptured along a fault line near Galway Lake. It created a spectacular escarpment seven to eight feet high and straight as a string for miles. It is awesome to see the force and power of Mother Nature. I shudder to think what would have happened if this had been a populated area!! This is a good camping area with lots of old mines to explore and views to enjoy.

Scouting Tips.........

Location: DeLorme page 96 A 4
Coordinates: GPS: N 34 degrees   32.037 W 116 degrees 33.201

Vehicle: 24WD

Lucerne Valley Leader Ad, Mar. 1, 1956
Courtesy of Mr. & Mrs. Bob McDougall

The Silver Cliff and Silver Bell silver mines

About ten miles north of the Bessemer Iron Mine and on the northeast slope of the Newberry Mountains, are two silver mines within walking distance of each other. Both have similar ore. Both mines are in rugged country and have extensive ruins. The ore is in dark red rock that cuts and polishes beautifully. At the Silver Bell there are ruins of a smelter with numerous concrete foundations and dwelling sites. At the Silver Cliff there is a huge wooden ore bin and ruins of a large mill. There is also a deep, open shaft that you should avoid. There are lots of interesting places to explore and beautiful places to camp. Please leave the ruins intact, so others can enjoy them. Enjoy!

Scouting Tips.........

Location: DeLorme page 83 C 4
Coordinates: GPS: N 34 degrees 42.067   W 116 degrees 29.932
Vehicle: 4 WD

The Silver Cliff and Silver Bell silver mines • 41

Lucerne Valley Leader Ad, Mar. 1, 1958 Courtesy of Mr. & Mrs. Bob McDougall

½ Alarm Fire

Fire Truck One from Engine Company One was called out Tuesday afternoon when the truck Charlie Scott was driving caught fire just East of the Miller Ranch on the 29 Palms highway.

The truck was damaged slightly when refuse in the back caught fire. The blaze was under control by the time the fire engine arrived.

Sand Dunes of Johnson Valley

MAP 22

At the bottom of Johnson Valley are a series of rolling sand dunes. They are beautiful, especially in the early morning and late afternoon, when they cast long and interesting shadows. This is a great family camping area. It is to be avoided when the wind is blowing. The kids will have a great time playing in this clean, fine sand. Please clean your campsite when you leave so others can have a good experience. Enjoy!

Scouting Tips.........

Location: Directions: DeLorme page 96 A 4
Coordinates: GPS: N 34 degrees 25.482   W 116 degrees 35.454
Directions: At 3.3 miles bear right. Follow the fence line 3.5 miles, turn left. Stay on the road. At 3.8 miles bear right the at 4.2 mile bear right again (at ruins of tank). Dunes are at 4.8 miles.

Vehicle: 4 WD

Emerson Gold Mine

Be careful! Open mine shafts can be very dangerous. Below; Author in front of old stone cabin.

West of Emerson Dry Lake is the Emerson Gold Mine. The last record of ownership was 1937, and the owner was Sarah Emerson of Hodge. The mine is in the mountains but the mill was on the southwest edge of Emerson Dry Lake. At the mine there is a fairly complete stone cabin besides other signs of habitation. There is lots of mining activity including a dangerous, deep shaft. There are posts with the name "Leprechaum" on them, put there by an unknown prospector. This area was mined off and on for a very long time. The last known production was 1938. A fun place to explore. Stay out of the mines and stay alive. Pack it in and pack it out. Enjoy!

Scouting Tips.........

Location: DeLorme page 97 A 5.5
Coordinates: GPS: N 34 degrees 26.886 W 116 degrees 26.808

Vehicle: 2WD High Clearance

Bessemer Iron Mines

Northwest of Galway Lake on the south slope of Iron Ridge, are the Bessemer Iron Mines. There are at least fourteen locations of deposits of iron ore. They have been mined and owned by various companies. The two main companies were Kaiser and Mineral Materials Co. of Alhambra, California. The ore was mainly shipped in the 1940's and 1950's involving many thousands of tons. The remote location, very distant from the nearest railroad, created a serious transportation problem. The high grade iron ore was shipped to Japan and sent to the local smelters. The lower grade was used as an additive in the making of cement. Other deposits have opened up around the world close to rail or ocean transport, and the mining at this location has become uneconomical. There are still large amounts of good ore here. There are interesting places to explore and beautiful places to camp. Since it is so remote, be prepared before you attempt to travel here. Enjoy!

Scouting Tips.........

Location: DeLorme page 83 D 4
Coordinates: GPS: N 34 degrees 34.880 W 116 degrees 33.735
Directions: Sixteen miles from Highway 247 to the mine. Good camping at the Rock Pile.
Vehicle: 2WD High Clearance

"Ironman" Don Taylor at the Bessemer Mine site.

Willie Boy's Grave

Willie Boy was a Paiute Indian that was twenty-seven years old in 1909, six feet tall, and was born in Pahrump, Nevada. He grew to manhood in Pahrump and married a woman of his tribe. He left Pahrump with his wife to look for work but returned a few months later without his wife. He never said anything about her absence but returned the wedding gifts to the donors. He left again to hunt for work and ended up in the Twenty-Nine Palms area where a distant relative, Old Mike Boniface, lived. Old Mike had a fourteen year old daughter named Lolita, and Willie Boy fell in love. Willie Boy asked Mike for permission to marry Lolita, but Mike refused. Mike said that it was against Indian custom to marry relatives even though the relationship was remote. Mike was working on a ranch in Banning at the time Willie Boy eloped with Lolita. Mike chased them down and, at gun point, returned Lolita home. Later, Willie Boy crept into Mike's house and with a rifle he had stolen, shot Mike in the head, killing him. He took off with Lolita and a bottle of whiskey. Willie Boy headed for the desert area that he was familiar with. He at one time had worked for the Heart Bar Ranch as a cowboy and knew where the springs were located. A posse was quickly formed and the chase was on. Lolita couldn't keep up the pace and when her strength gave out, Willie Boy shot her. He feared, if she were caught, she would have been badly mistreated by her family. The posse finally cornered Willie Boy in some boulders. A gunfight occurred in which three of the horses of the posse were shot and one man, named Richie, was badly wounded. When Willie Boy was down to his last bullet, he committed suicide. The posse cremated him on the spot and thus ended this sad saga. The press of the day added greatly to this sensational story and a movie was even made of it.

Jan Lembright at Willy Boy's grave.

Scouting Tips.........
Location: DeLorme page 97 B 4
Coordinates: GPS: N 34 degrees 17.497 W 116 degrees 32.194
Vehicle: Vehicle: 4 WD

46 • Bill Mann's Guide to the Lucerne Valley

Integratron

MAP 26

why isn't this boy in school?

Art by Rocky Johnson

Integratron • 47

Nancy Karl explaining the Integratron

Of all the sites in this book, I believe the Integratron is the most mysterious and interesting. I strongly recommend that everyone visit the Integratron and get a sound bath by the gracious Nancy Karl. Nancy and her sister, Joanne Karl, own the Integratron, and are hostesses for your tour. They gave us a remarkable tour which I will never forget. Read the information in the brochures they gave us and be prepared for a visit you will never forget. Gublers Orchids is within sight with a nice picnic area. Giant Rock is nearby.

Scouting Tips.........

Location: DeLorme page 97 B 5
Coordinates: GPS: N 34 degrees 17.652 W 116 degrees 24.162
Directions: Corner of Bellfield Road and Linn Road.

Vehicle: 2WD

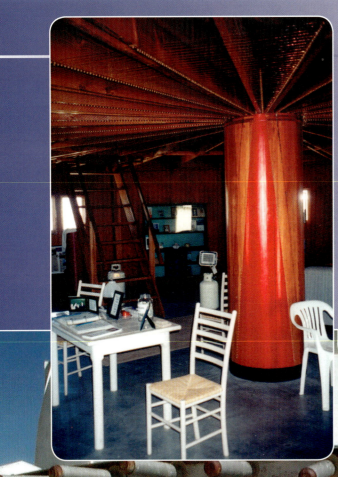
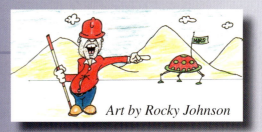

Art by Rocky Johnson

Above; Nancy Karl readies for delivery of sound bath. Below, Nancy, Joanne and the Author outside the Integratron.

Giant Rock

Paul and Rene Longshore with Author and Derald Francis at Giant Rock

Northerly from Landers, on the edge of a small, ancient playa, is a very famous, huge granite boulder. And I mean huge! It covers over 5000 square feet of ground space and is five or six stories high. The weight is unknown thousands of tons. In 1930, a World War I German submarine veteran named Frank Critzer decided to become a prospector, picking Giant Rock as his base camp. He filed a mining claim on it and began digging out a two room home under the rock. The home was very comfortable, being cool in the summer and warm in the winter. Frank had a radio antenna on top of the boulder. Being German, he drew the suspicion of authorities at the beginning of World War II. In 1942, three Riverside authorities arrived to question him and he said "just a minute". A tremendous explosion occurred that killed Frank and injured the three deputies. No one, to this day, knows exactly what happened. A friend of Frank's, named George Van Tassel took a lease on the property and moved in. He had been a test pilot for Howard Hughes. After moving in, he improved a dirt landing strip alongside the boulder. One summer night, while sleeping outside under the stars, he was awakened by a UFO that hovered over him. They were from Venus and friendly. They beamed him up into the spacecraft and gave him the plans to the Integraton. He published this episode and set off a craze about UFO's. In 1954, he held his first Giant Rock Convention which became the first of seventeen annual conventions. The Intregraton will be in another story. George Van Tassel died in 1978, taking many a story with him. Unfortunately, Giant Rock has been badly vandalized. A large chunk split off by itself. But what a story it could tell if it could talk! It is a great place to camp and if you are luckily, you might even get beamed up! Enjoy!

Scouting Tips.........

Location: DeLorme page 97 B 5.5
Coordinates: GPS: N 34 degrees 19.908   W 116 degrees 23.225
Directions: Take Belfield Rd. to end. Turn right on Linn (dirt road), immediately fork left. Follow to next fork (approx. 2 miles) then fork right, follow Belfield painted on rock.
Vehicle: 2WD

50 • Bill Mann's Guide to the Lucerne Valley

Gubler Orchids

Scouting Tips..........

Location: DeLorme page 97 B 5
Coordinates: GPS: N 34 degrees 17.221 W 116 degrees 24.131

Vehicle: 2WD

All photos by Steven Rohn

Gubler Orchids • 51

Near the corner of Belfield Blvd. and Linn Road in Landers, are a series of large, nondescript metal buildings. This is the home of the world famous Gubler Orchid Co. They have over a million orchids of all shapes and sizes as well as carnivorous plants. The orchids are exported around the world but mainly in Canada and the United States. What an awesome surprise to come out of the desert, enter these buildings, and be greeted by a mass of beautiful, blooming orchids. Heinrich Gubler started his nursery in Switzerland in 1918 and quickly expanded. He moved to the United States in 1949, and after trying several locations, settled in Landers. Now his son, Chris, runs the business. It is within sight of the Integratron and both can be seen on the same trip. Both are a must! Enjoy!

Dottie "Dynamite" Mann in one of Gubler's greenhouses

Johnson Valley Petroglyphs and Booths' Folly

High on the north slope of the San Bernardino Mountains, near the head of Yaranka Canyon, (an Indian word for desert or desertlike), are the Johnson Valley Petroglyphs. As the canyon narrows, the petroglyphs are on either side. These are precious examples of "rock art" created hundreds of years ago. No one knows for sure why the ancient ones created this art, but it is for us to enjoy and protect. Please don't touch them, because the oil in your hands could damage them. Remember: it is a serious federal crime to damage or remove Indian relics. Take nothing but pictures and leave nothing but footprints. Enjoy!

Author beside Petroglyph. Opposite page; Author and Bill Wilson at Booth's Folly.

Scouting Tips.........

Location: DeLorme page 97 B 4.5
Coordinates: GPS: N 34 degrees 19.788 W 116 degrees 32.136
Vehicle: Vehicle: 4 WD

Johnson Valley Petroglyphs and Booths Folly • 53

Booths Folly is at the beginning or mouth of Yaranka Canyon. It is an odd house or building built of rock and cement. It is perched atop a point of rock overlooking the beginning of Yaranka Canyon. Whoever built it went to a lot of trouble and hard work, but ended up with an awesome view. We don't know its exact age, but it is at least fifty years old. It is in a sandy area, so be careful about getting stuck. A great area to camp, great views, and spectacular rock formations. We have Bill Wilson to thank for showing us these two sites. Enjoy!

Lucerne Valley Leader Ad, Jan. 10, 1957 Courtesy of Mr. & Mrs. Bob McDougall

54 • Bill Mann's Guide to the Lucerne Valley

Rock Corral

MAP 30

In the foothills of the San Bernardino Mountains near Landers, the Swarthout Cattle Company developed in the early 1900's, a small spring. They ran the water into a cattle trough inside a large corral made of large boulders. Some of these boulders must have weighed over half a ton, and how they hoisted them up, I'll never know. They have made an impressive landmark. It is a pretty place to camp with a large tree for shade and running water. Please leave the area cleaner than when you found it, and maybe we won't have so many restrictions. Enjoy!

Scouting Tips.........

Location: DeLorme page 97 B 4
Coordinates: GPS: N 34 degrees 19.394 W 116 degrees 33.597
Vehicle: 2WD High Clearance

Rock Corral/Old Woman Springs • 55

MAP 31
Old Woman Springs...more...

O ld Woman Springs is a major spring area in the Johnson Valley alongside Highway 247. In 1856, a government surveying party found several elderly Indian women living at the Springs and officially named it "Old Woman Springs". It has appeared on government maps ever since. There is lots of evidence that it was used a very long time by the local Indians. The incoming ranchers found many metates and other grinding artifacts. Albert Swarthout homesteaded Old Woman Springs in 1907. He first homesteaded in Lucerne Valley around 1893, and established the Box S cattle ranch. He soon found that area would not support enough cattle for a successful ranch, so he looked elsewhere, and settled on the Old Woman Springs area. He took for his cattle brand a heart with a

Scouting Tips.........

Location: DeLorme page 96 A 3
Vehicle: 2WD

bar under it. Thus, the Hart Bar Ranch.

The Old Woman Springs area was good for cattle most of the year, but summers were too hot, and the cattle were driven into the mountains near Big Bear for the summer season. Albert, or Swarthy, as his friends called him, had a partner named Gentry. As most partnerships work, they had a falling out and dissolved their partnership in 1947. Gentry took most of the desert property and Swarthout took the mountain property. This ended the many years of Swarthout occupation at Old Woman Springs.

Gentry imported a small work train and ten miles of track from a pineapple ranch in Hawaii. It was his hobby for a few years. The train is gone, the cattle are gone, and a new era of homesteading and desert living arrived.

Old Woman Springs is a beautiful reparian area with two lakes and year round water fowl.

High above Old Woman Springs is a beautiful granite monument to the King of Lucerne Valley, his two daughters and son. They all burned to death in 1978.

It is private property with no trespassing signs but private tours can be arranged by calling Bob Humphrey at 760-217-7126 . He asks for a small donation to cover his expenses. The property at this writing, is for sale. Enjoy!

Peaceful bliss at Old Woman Springs

Avelardo Guajardo, self proclaimed "King of Lucerne Valley" and family rests peacefully at Old Woman Springs.

Bob Humphrey with Author at Old Woman Springs

Lester Dale Mine

High on the north slope of the San Bernardino Mountains is the Lester Dale Mine. It is a very well preserved mining camp. It had a very good water system that still works today. The buildings are in good condition. In the front yard are some large, fenced grape vines showing that people lived here for a very long time. The gold is in two quartz veins high on the side of the mountain to the northwest of the camp. It was rumored that the Spanish had taken some gold out of this deposit in the old, old days. Most production was in the 1920's although some gold was produced as late as 1952. There is a well preserved mill still there. The huge white quarry behind the Lester Dale is the Partin Limestone Quarry which is not active as of May, 2003. This is a great place to explore with awesome views. Please respect the property so others can enjoy it. Enjoy!

Area highlighted below shows Lester Dale Mine location, just below the Partin Limestone Quarry

Scouting Tips.........

Location: DeLorme page 96 B 2
Coordinates: GPS: N 34 degrees 20.262 W 116 degrees 46.400
Vehicle: 2WD High Clearance

All photos by Renee and Paul Longshore

Stone buildings and mining camp

The spring at Lester Dale camp.

Blackhawk Gold Mine and Mill

MAP 33

The Blackhawk Mine is in Blackhawk Canyon on the north slope of the San Bernardino Mountains between three thousand and six thousand feet. It consists of many tunnels and shafts some requiring tramways (one about a mile long) to bring ore to the mill. The Blackhawk Gold Mining Co. was first formed in 1888, and a ten stamp mill was built. It operated for about two years. Then the price of gold dropped and the mill was removed. The mine remained idle for almost thirty years.

Mining was renewed in the early 1920's by a mining engineer named Algernon Del Mar. It was carried on and off through the depression. In World War II it was shut down. After World War II, in the 1980's, the price of gold climbed to a record high of $850 per ounce and mining resumed. A road was blasted up the canyon and a large mill was built at the mouth of the canyon. A three and a half mile long, five inch in diameter water line was installed bringing in plenty of water from Arrastra Creek. The price of gold fell and once again the mine and mill became idle. This is a beautiful area to explore but be careful around the ruins and mines. There are lots of big diamond back snakes. Enjoy!

Scouting Tips.........

Location: DeLorme page 96 B 2
Coordinates: GPS: N 34 degrees 21.62
 W 116 degrees 47.711
Vehicle: 2WD High Clearance

Art by Rocky Johnson

Blackhawk Gold Mine and Mill/Blackhawk Land Slide • 61

Blackhawk Land Slide

Over 18,000 years ago, one of the largest landslides in the world occurred here in Lucerne Valley. After a period of several years of heavy rainfall, which soaked the area, an earthquake of over eight on the earthquake scale, shook the area. A huge area split off from the north slope of the San Bernardino Mountains and roared out into the desert. The slide covers approximately five and a half square miles, and rode out onto the desert on a cushion of air traveling an estimated two hundred miles per hour. What an awesome event! Good views and camping in the area. If you feel the ground shake, run for cover! Enjoy!

Scouting Tips.........

Location: DeLorme page 96 A 2
Coordinates: GPS N34° 25.618, W116° 47.388
Vehicle: 2WD

John Masse, Derald Francis, Jan and Bill Lembright survey the Blackhawk slide

Silver Reef Mine

On the north slope of the San Bernardino Mountains and just west of Partin Limestone Road, is the Silver Reef Mine. The mine consists of many tunnels, shafts, and open pits. There are many buildings still standing, just pleading to be explored. There has been activity here off and on since before 1900. It has been idle since the 1950's. Please be careful with fire as some buildings have already been burned down. Leave them so others can enjoy them. A good place to camp with great views of the valley. Enjoy!

Scouting Tips.........

Location: DeLorme page 96 A 2.5
Coordinates: GPS: N 34 degrees 22.540 W 116 degrees 45.099
Vehicle: 2WD High Clearance

Silver Reef Mine/Lucerne Valley Bits • 63

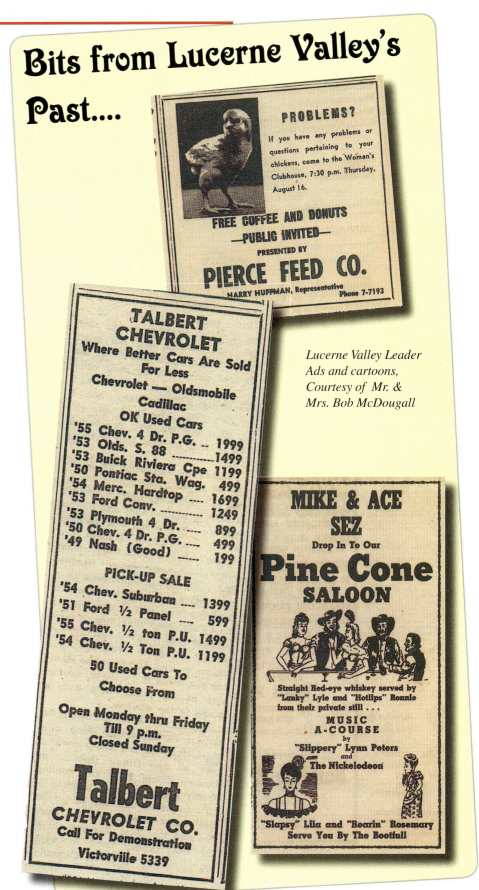

Bits from Lucerne Valley's Past....

Lucerne Valley Leader Ads and cartoons, Courtesy of Mr. & Mrs. Bob McDougall

Hot Glass Ranch

MAP 36

Don Taylor and I were treated to a tour of Jon Bush's glass blowing and art facilities. We were greeted by Jon's gracious wife, Becky, and then Jon took over the tour. His furnaces were roaring, but he still gave us a great tour. Lucerne Valley is indeed fortunate to have someone as talented as Jon. His works are breathtaking and famous throughout the country. They are sold in prestigious galleries and stores from Palm Springs to Minnesota. Don and I were very impressed by the quality of his work. He even recycles some of the excess heat from his furnaces to a nursery he has at his ranch. Jon cannot be interrupted at his ranch because time is critical when he is melting or blowing glass. He gives tours but a reservation must be made by phone and drop ins are not welcome. His phone number is: 760-248-9644. Enjoy!

Scouting Tips.........

Location: 11180 Post Office Road

Vehicle: 2WD

Hot Glass Ranch/Gobar's Dairy • 65

MAP 37 — Gobar's Dairy

Julian Gobar, his friends called him Junie, was one of Lucerne Valley's early pioneers. He came in the early 1900's and established a dairy not far from the southern edge of Lucerne Dry Lake on Gobar Road. His ranch house and dairy buildings are abandoned, but still there. It is like a trip into the past to see them. Please don't disturb anything, so people can enjoy these relics for many years to come. Enjoy!

Scouting Tips..........

Location: DeLorme page 96 A 1
Coordinates: GPS: N 34 degrees 27.955
            W 116 degrees 56.782
Vehicle: 2WD

Rabbit Springs and the Hangman Tree

Rabbit Springs is a beautiful riparian area right alongside Rabbit Springs Road. It is private property owned by the John Ligouri family. Rabbit Springs was created by a large, underground fault causing the water to be blocked and rise to the surface. It was inhabited for unknown thousands of years by early Americans because of the abundance of game and edible plants such as mesquite beans. It was the home of Peter Davidson, the first Caucasian settler in the area. The first justice of the peace was there. It was reputed that justice was swift and severe for cattle rustlers and horse thieves. A huge, old cottonwood still stands, and was supposedly used to carry out the sentences. Peter had built a supply station to service the travelers that went by on the wagon road. Please respect the privacy of the Ligouri family. They are good people and were very helpful to me. You can get a good look from Rabbit Springs Road. Enjoy!

Rabbit Springs and the Hangman Tree • 67

Mr. and Mrs. John Ligouri

Scouting Tips.........

Location: DeLorme page 96 A 1
Coordinates: GPS: N 34 degrees 27.495
W 116 degrees 57.762
Vehicle: 2WD High Clearance

Another Desperado bites the dust!

Peter Davidson's Grave

At a jog in Rabbit Springs Road, just west of Rabbit Springs, is the grave of Peter Davidson. He was the first Caucasian settler in the area. He lived at Rabbit Springs for many years. He set up a small way station, where he sold supplies to the travelers passing through on the nearby wagon road. He was well liked. When law came to the area he was the first Justice of the Peace. As far as I can determine, he never married, but was a kind of Godfather to many in the area. May he rest in peace!

Scouting Tips.........

Location: DeLorme page 96 A
Coordinates: GPS: N 34 degrees 27.492
W116 degrees 57.995
Vehicle: 2WD

Box S Ranch

The Box S Ranch, in the middle of Lucerne Valley, was originally homesteaded by Albert R. Swarthout in the early 1890's. He was going to run cattle on the homestead but the lack of water and grass prevented him from doing so. While Swarthout was looking for other grazing land, as well as working for the Forest Service, a squatter moved onto this Lucerne Valley homestead. His name was James "Dad" Goulding. Swarthout gave up his claim and the two men became friends. Goulding put down a well that produced pure water and became very successful. He put in a store, and became a bitter competitor to "Uncle Pete" Davidson. Goulding lived to be ninety-nine, and was dominant for many years in improving Lucerne Valley. Little remains of the Box S Ranch today, just a chimney and some concrete slabs. Plus lots of memories and maybe a few ghosts. Enjoy!

Scouting Tips.........

Location: DeLorme page 96 A 1
Address: 32607 Hwy 18 (downtown Lucerne Valley)
Vehicle: 2WD

Rancho El Sueno and The El Sueno Arrastra

MAP 41

Just off Highway 18, leading up into the San Bernardino Mountains, are the ruins of El Sueno guest ranch.

In the 1940's and into the 1960's it was a well respected and prosperous guest ranch where city people could come to the high desert, bask in the sun, ride horseback and swim in their beautiful out door swimming pool. The hosts were Ruth and Les Clark. As the years went by, the popularity of these guest ranches dropped off and sadly, Rancho El Sueno was abandoned and fell into ruins. It is sad to see such a fun place in a terrible state of disrepair. Behind El Sueno at a small gold mine, reputed to be owned by the Holcomb brothers, is one of the most well preserved arrastras I have ever seen. I know you will marvel over it as I did. Enjoy!

Jan and Bill Lembright stand in the Arrastra.

Scouting Tips........

Location: DeLorme page 96 A 1.5
Coordinates: GPS: N 34 degrees 23.803
              W 116 degrees 53.666
Vehicle: 2WD

Above; Rancho El Sueno dining room. Left; a promotional brochure. Below; a view of Rancho El Sueno

Wolf Mountain Sanctuary

MAP 42

High on the north slope of the San Bernardino Mountains just off Highway 18, is a sign of a howling wolf. This is the home of Tonya Littlewolf and her adopted wolves. Tonya is a remarkable Apache lady, with a lifelong passion for wolves. She takes in wolves about to be destroyed because they can no longer be cared for and desperately need a home. She gives them both food and love, and makes them available for the public to view. She has formed a non-profit corporation. Tonya is seeking help to provide food and lodging for her beloved wolves.

You can go in a double fenced cage and play with the tamer wolves. I love critters and got a special thrill in interacting with these beautiful animals. She also asks a nominal donation for you to pet these wolves. I would like the public to help her in her goal to save the wolf from extinction. I think you would have a good time visiting Tonya and her wolves. Enjoy!

Tonya, Jan Lembright and one of the magnificent wolves in Tonyas' care.

Scouting Tips.........

Location: DeLorme page 96 A 1
Coordinates: GPS: N 34 degrees 23.375
                        W 116 degrees 52.532
Vehicle: 2WD

Cushenbury Springs

MAP 43

John Cushenbury, a prospector and miner in 1860, discovered silver in the limestone deposit that Mitsubishi is now mining. He set up a mining camp at the springs below his deposit. As word got out about his discovery, a minor silver rush occurred. A small group of shacks was built in the vicinity of the springs. It was called "Cushenbury City". Unfortunately, the silver contained galena, or lead, and was hard to separate. The boom turned to a bust and most of the miners moved on. The Civil War began, and many miners in the area had confederate sympathies. They met secretly at Cushenbury to plan how they could help the confederacy. These miners were called "The Knights of the Golden Circle". They planted a circle of seventeen cottonwood trees which stand today.

Scouting Tips.........

Location: DeLorme page 96 B 1
Coordinates: GPS: N 34 degrees 21.718
W 116 degrees 51.435
Vehicle: 2WD

The Springs are a large, beautiful reparian area alongside Highway 18, just before you get to the Mitsubishi Cement Plant. The area is a very historic spot. It was inhabited by Indians, then miners, and for years a large turkey and chicken ranch operated by George Rodgers. Rodgers sold the ranch to the cement company. They removed the buildings in the 1960's. The main ranch home was moved to Daggett to the Muir Ranch. I have Doug Schumway, Environmental Manager of the Mitsubishi Cement Co., to thank for most of this information. He asks that you be careful due to heavy traffic on Highway 18, but otherwise you are welcome to visit the property. Enjoy!

Dave Fisher, (l.), and Billy Mitchell (r.) are the two remaining cattle ranchers in the Lucerne Valley area

Granite Mountain Railroad

MAP 44

The large red buildings northerly from the intersection of Rabbit Springs Road and Highway 18, are the home of Granite Mountain Railroad. When Knott's Berry Farm in Anaheim decided to do away with their miniature railroad because of liability and other problems, longtime Knott railroad employee and maintenance manager, Chuck Valenzuela, and his wife, Marjorie, bought the little railroad and moved it "lock, stock, and barrel" to Lucerne Valley. They are collectors of railroad memorabilia and antiques. They built several buildings to house their collections. Chuck also built a large machine shop to store and repair his railroad stock. He laid down track in several large circles going over bridges and through tunnels. The track goes past a depression era gas station.

He has done a great job in meticulously restoring his beloved railroad stock. Marge takes great pride in showing her collection of antique toys and glassware.

The Granite Mountain Railroad is often rented as a movie location. Although it is not open to the public, it is available for private tours. The Valenzuelas are gracious hosts and can be contacted for private tours by calling 760-964-2684. Enjoy this treasure of Lucerne Valley!

Scouting Tips........
Location: DeLorme page 95 A 7
Coordinates: GPS: N 34 degrees 27.428
                          W 117 degrees 00.398
Vehicle: 2WD

Left to right; John Masse, Marjorie Valenzuela, Derald Francis, Julie Clemmer, the Author and Engineer Chuck Valenzuela aboard the Granite Mountain Railroad.

Granite Mountain Railroad • 77

Author with Marjorie and Chuck Valenzuela

TA-4J Aircraft Crash Site

High on the west slope of upper Lovelace Canyon is the widely scattered wreckage of a Navy training attack jet. In 1970, the jet experienced a burn out and was too low for the pilot to be able to restart the engine. The pilot safely ejected and parachuted down to Rabbit Dry Lake. The plane continued on at high speed for several miles, missing a remote solitary house, and exploding into a thousand pieces upon contact with the ground. A one hundred fifty acre brush fire ensued. The landing gear legs are near the site with pieces of the fuselage scattered between landing gear and the dry wash far below. I have Al Miller and Bill Lembright to thank for this information. Enjoy!

Pat Eblen points to part of the A-4's landing gear

Scouting Tips.........

Location: DeLorme page 95 A 7
Coordinates: GPS: N 34 degrees 23.700 W 117 degrees 04.911
Directions: 7.4 miles west of four way stop on Highway 18, left on Lovelace Canyon Road for 1.8 miles to BNSF RR track crossing, continue south (or straight ahead) for .9 more miles, veer right on to the power line road, drive for .7 miles past two dirt roads, then turn left for .4 mile. Park on the graded spot next to the fence corner above Lovelace Canyon's west boundary. Hike 1.3 miles on well traveled motorcycle trail that travels the south ridge of Lovelace Canyon and passes within one hundred feet of the landing gear.

Vehicle: 2WD High Clearance

Verde Antique Marble Quarries

In the north Lucerne Valley area, and southwest of the Lucerne Valley cutoff road, are a series of small, unique quarries. These quarries have mainly been worked by amateur rockhounds looking for cutting and polishing material. The marble is unusual because it was once crushed in the earth's crust and then resolidified. Each outcrop is a different color. When cut and polished, it is very beautiful. A beautiful area to camp with awesome views. Enjoy!

Author takes a break on a marble boulder

Gary Grant of Barstow made the marble sphere and bookends pictured below

Scouting Tips.........

Location: DeLorme page 81 C 7
Coordinates: GPS: N 34 degrees 37.677
        W 116 degrees 03.368
Vehicle: 2WD

On the north slope of the San Bernardino Mountains and in the San Bernardino National Forest are a series of hot springs alongside Deep Creek. These hot springs are very isolated and are on government land. As of May, 2003, they are still open but overnight camping and campfires are prohibited. The hot water seeps into pools and mixes with the cold stream water. You can pick your temperatures as they vary from very hot to cold and everything in between. The springs are in a rather rocky, narrow, but scenic canyon. The best way to get to them is to park near the Bowen Ranch and hike in. It is not a long hike (about a mile or two) but very steep. Mike Castro, an accomplished artist and my friend, owns Bowen Ranch and charges a modest four dollars to cross his property, park on his property, clean the trail, and monitor the area. He is strict but loves the area and is reasonable to deal with. I appeal to people to keep the area clean and peaceful and maybe we can avoid oppressive regulations. Enjoy!

Deep Creek Hot Springs

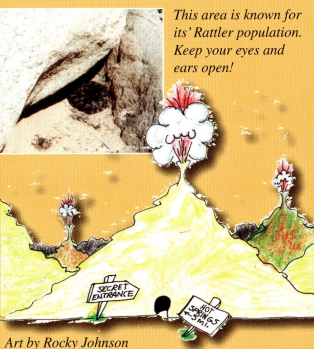

This area is known for its' Rattler population. Keep your eyes and ears open!

Art by Rocky Johnson

Scouting Tips.........

Location: DeLorme page 95 B 6
Coordinates: GPS: N 34 degrees 20.408
W 117 degrees 10.653
Vehicle: 2WD

Lucerne Dry Lake Earthquake Cracks

MAP 48a

On the far west side of Lucerne Dry Lake are a series of deep earthquake cracks. Some are ten to twelve feet wide and deep enough so you can't see the bottom. They are very spectacular and show the power and furry of Mother Nature.

Enjoy!

Jan Lembright (right) and Author (below) check the massive cracks

Earthquake Cracks and Rocket Site location...

Scouting Tips.........

Location: DeLorme page 96 A 1
Coordinates: GPS: N 34 degrees 30.300
                        W 116 degrees 58.642
Vehicle: 2WD High Center

Lucerne Dry Lake Rocket Site

The second Saturday of each month, ROC (Rocketry Organization of California) holds a meet. Members shoot off their rockets under a controlled and safe environment. These members are amateurs and these rockets range from small to some twelve to fourteen feet tall. Twice each year, in June and November, there is a national meet where the big rockets are shot and are very spectacular. They are shot into the air thousands of feet and they must get FAA clearance. Everyone must see at least one of these meets. Maybe you'll get hooked on rockets! Enjoy!

Author and Rocketeer beside models awaiting turn for launch pad

Dinosaur House

Prior to restoration by the Boy Scouts

Alongside the Lucerne Valley cut-off road in north Lucerne Valley is a very strange site indeed. It is a single wide mobile home wrapped with stucco wire with a long tail and a tall, large dinosaur head made with telephone poles. It is covered with Plaster of Paris and is painted blue green. Lucerne Valley has its own Tyranosorous Rex dinosaur!

This creation was the work of Joe Whitcavitch, a life long telephone lineman born in Vermont. Joe loved to tinker and made weird things. He drove a vehicle with the front a VW and the rear of another make car. In 1985, Joe moved to Lucerne Valley, bought ten acres of remote desert land, and went to work on his dinosaur. He loved his remote home and tinkered with many projects. When he went to town and entered a store, he would let out a loud howl, and some of the locals would howl back.

Scouting Tips.........

Location: DeLorme page 82 C 1
Directions: Approximately 1.4 miles west of Highway 247 on Lucerne Valley Cut Off Road
Vehicle: 2WD

Dinosaur House • 85

Author with daughter Janice and grandson, Eddie Chagoya

Sadly, Joe's life was cut short in a vehicle rollover and his body was returned to Vermont. I am sure his soul rests with his beloved dinosaur. Joe's dinosaur has been badly vandalized and trashed. The Boy Scouts, Troop 247 of Lucerne Valley and Troop 62 of Barstow, agreed to take on the job of clean up and restoration. Doug Shumway of Mitsubishi Cement Company removed the trash. Joe's dinosaur is nearing final restoration and now we can all enjoy his dream. We have his heirs' permission to do this project. Enjoy!

Lucerne Valley's Annual Great American Worm Race

Every May for the last four years, there has been an annual worm race. It takes place at the Lucerne Valley High School. Everyone has a great time and this past year $1200 was raised for local charities. This is how it works: the worms are donated and for ten dollars you can buy a worm, name it, then enter it in the race. It is great fun. I entered one named Shortfuse but alas, Shortfuse didn't even show, finishing out of the money. The last I heard, he was on his way to a bait shop at Big Bear Lake. Be sure you don't miss the worm race next May!

See you at the Worm Race!!!

Sawtooth Canyon

MAP 51

On the north side of Goat Pass and west of Highway 247, is Sawtooth Canyon. The canyon divides like a Y with two arms. The right arm has a spring that has, in the wet time of the year, a small gurgling brook through scenic pools and grottos. The left fork goes up a canyon of awesome rock formations which a rock climbing club has named New Jack City. That is what NJC stands for. They have put posts and benches in the area where you can sit and watch the rock climbers in action. In the middle of the Y is a huge rock formation called "the Rockpile". The ancient people also used the Rockpile area for camping. I counted five bedrock metates (grinding slabs) and one small faint pictograph. It is a beautiful, scenic camping area. Pack it in, pack it out. Enjoy!

Author with one of the bedrock metates

Scouting Tips.........

Location: DeLorme page 81 C 7
Coordinates: GPS: N 34 degrees 48.136
W 116 degrees 58.972
Vehicle: 2WD

Goat Mountain

Goat Mountain is just to the east of Goat Pass, halfway between Barstow and Lucerne Valley on Highway 247. If you view Goat Mountain from the north to the south, you should see a goat lying down with his eye open. The signs were placed there by Will and Darlene Garrett. See if you can find the Goat. A few beers might help. Enjoy!

Author with Will Garrett trying to find the goat

MAP 53

The Lucerne Valley Museum

The Lucerne Valley Museum is located on Highway 247, one quarter mile east of the junction of Highway 247 and Highway 18 and adjoining Pioneer Park. It is a great museum with an outstanding outdoor selection of antique mining and farming equipment. The museum is open by appointment only until they can find a permanent docent to keep it open fulltime. You can view the outside displays through the chain link fence. Phone is 760-964-2684. The address is P.O. Box 1762. The museum is struggling financially and any donations would be gratefully accepted.

Bill Lembright and Author await bail.

Art by Rocky Johnson

Chimney Rock

Chimney Rock is an enormous spectacular rock formation north of Rabbit Dry Lake. It was a landmark on the nearby wagon road. The desert Indians of the area would occasionally go down through the mountains and raid the ranchos of horses and cattle, often taking hostages. In the winter of 1866-67, the Indians mounted a major raid carrying off horses and cattle and, as the story goes, a young woman. The ranchers, not taking this lightly, formed a large posse, tracked them to the vicinity, and trapped a large group, including the woman, in a large rock shelter on the back side of chimney rock. During the gun battle, a young Indian, braving gun fire, hurried the young woman to safety and left her behind a rock near the lake. She was found there by members of her family. The gun battle was on February 16, 1867. It left many Indians dead or wounded. This was the last major battle between the Indians and the settlers of the area. If that rock formation could talk, what a story it could tell. Enjoy!

Scouting Tips.........

Location: DeLorme page 95 A 7
Coordinates: GPS: N 34 degrees 28.076
                  W 117 degrees 01.201
Vehicle: 2WD

Chimney Rock/Hitchhiker's Thumb • 91

Hitchhiker's Thumb

MAP 55

In the western part of Lucerne Valley, close to highway 18, in a picturesque little grotto among huge granite boulders, is a small rock formation called Hitchhiker's Thumb.

I think Mother Nature created the Hitchhiker's Thumb to prove she has a sense of humor. I really enjoy this little formation and I hope you do too. Enjoy.

Scouting Tips..........

Location: DeLorme page 95 A 7
Coordinates: GPS Coordinates   N 34 degrees 29.326   W 117 degrees   08.177
Vehicle: 2WD

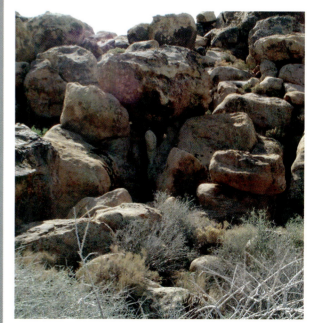

The Desert in Bloom

LUCERNE VALLEY MARKET AND ACE HARDWARE
YOUR COMPLETE SHOPPING CENTER

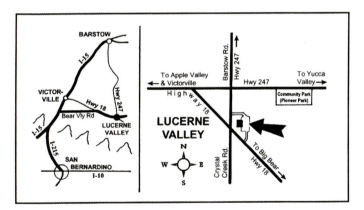

Here in the center of Lucerne Valley is a large, modern general store. A sampling:

- groceries
- fresh meat and produce
- the Deli Cafe
  - breakfast & other great sandwiches
  - subs
  - superburgers
  - deep fried or rotisserie chicken
  - salads
  - soft ice cream
  - fountain drinks
- beverages
- liquor
- greeting cards
- health and beauty items
- Ace hardware
  - 25,000 items
  - unusual stuff like gold pans, washboards, wood stoves
- RV supplies
- camping, fishing, & hunting items
- firewood
- automotive, motorcycle, & bicycle stuff
- models
- cameras & film
- batteries
- ATM's at each checkstand

BOOKS • • • • BOOKS • • • • BOOKS
- Bill Mann's guide books
- Lots of other books about the area
- More books of all kinds

ALMOST ANYTHING ELSE you can think of.
ACCEPTING ALL MAJOR CREDIT CARDS

AND AT THIS SHOPPING CENTER
- Full service bank (real people) with 24 hour ATM
- Coin laundry
- Beauty shop
- Recycling station

Bill Lembright, Ernie Gommel and Linda Gommel welcome you.

WELCOME TO BEAUTIFUL LUCERNE VALLEY

Mitsubishi Cement Corp is proud to be a steward of the land. The Cushenbury Plant has preserved riparian habitat in the Cushenbury Springs and the revegetation work in the mine is successfully re-establishing native plant communities disturbed by mining operations.

After trekking through the sites around Lucerne Valley, rest your feet, cool your head and feed your belly with the finest in steak, ribs and cold beer.

Stop and see us, you won't leave hungry!

Author with owner, Dave Krumbine and daughter Tina Bilby who will welcome you to Slash X Ranch.

Sunset over Lucerne Valley • Photo by Clifford Palmer

Thank you for visiting
LUCERNE VALLEY

Author and daughter Julie Clemmer thank you for visiting Lucerne Valley and hope you will come back

Lucerne Valley Gallery

Courtesy of Chuck Rader

ART MC CALL holding bobcat he killed in his chicken house after the cat slaughtered 525 fryers.

Lucerne Valley Leader, Dec 6, 1956
Courtesy of Mr. & Mrs. Bob McDougall

Courtesy of Donna Chandler

Lucerne Valley Gallery • 99

Courtesy of Chuck Rader

Lucerne Valley Leader Ad, August 15, 1957
Courtesy of Mr. & Mrs. Bob McDougall

Courtesy of Mojave River Valley Museum

Lucerne Valley Leader Ad, April 26, 1956 Courtesy of Mr. & Mrs. Bob McDougall

Courtesy of Dick Clark

Courtesy of Chuck Rader

Courtesy of Chuck Rader

Lucerne Valley Gallery • 101

Courtesy of Victor Valley College

Courtesy of Donna Chandler

102 • Bill Mann's Guide to the Lucerne Valley

Courtesy of Carolyn Russell

Photos Courtesy of Mojave River Valley Museum

Lucerne Valley Gallery • 103

All photos Courtesy of Mojave River Valley Museum

All photos Courtesy of Mojave River Valley Museum

Lucerne Valley Gallery • 105

All photos Courtesy of Mojave River Valley Museum

All photos Courtesy of Mojave River Valley Museum

Lucerne Valley Gallery

All photos Courtesy of Mojave River Valley Museum

ABOUT THE AUTHOR

I was born in Kansas on Dec. 30, 1926 and moved to California in 1929. I have two brothers.

Once, my father was asked to temporarily take over an ailing Boy Scout troop. This "temporary" job turned out to be a life-long commitment. It introduced me to hiking and camping, but most importantly, to the Mojave Desert. All three boys and dad became Eagle Scouts. Scouting has really enhanced my life.

In June, 1944, I graduated from Pomona High School followed by service in the U.S. Merchant Marines for two years. In service, I had a "distinguished" career as a cook and baker on a small, grubby, assault ammunitions ship assigned to the Marine Corps. We made five landings to provide ammunition during the war and one after the war to Northern China. It was an experience that taught me to enjoy every day of life.

After the war, I returned to graduate with an A.A. from Mount San Antonio College. I then entered Pomona College in Claremont and graduated in 1952 with a B.A. in history. During this time, I prowled the desert, camping, exploring and prospecting.

After graduation from Pomona College, I co-founded with my cousin, Ron Brubaker, Brubaker-Mann, Inc.. It is a mining company that produces specialty rock products and now I am the sole owner and still involved with this company after forty-nine years.

Because of my life-long love of history and the desert, I served for twelve years on the San Bernardino County Museum Commission and as chairman of that board for two years. I also became a charter member of The Mojave River Valley Museum in Barstow, served two terms as president and was on the board for many years. I have led museum field trips for over twenty one years.

I am currently serving as Wild Life Representative on the San Bernardino County RIAC board—a board that relates to cattle grazing issues in the desert.

An avid camper in the desert for more than fifty years, I am a fierce protector of the desert. I am married to my best friend and have one son and four daughters.